A 3-minute forever book

EAT YOUR PEAS®

Girlfriend

By Cheryl Karpen

Illustrated by Sandy Fougner

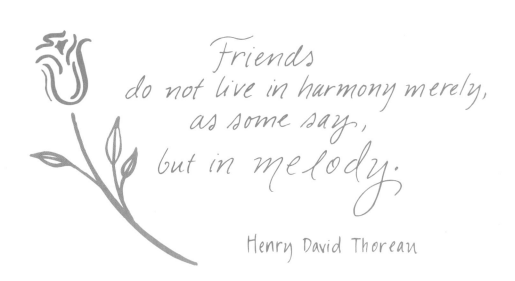

Friends
do not live in harmony merely,
as some say,
but in melody.

Henry David Thoreau

To _____

in celebration of our

friendship

with love from _____

At the
heart of this little book
is a promise.
It's a promise from me
to you
and it goes like this:

Whenever
you'd like a friend to
laugh with, cry with, vent to,
brag to or celebrate with...
Call me.

I promise
to be the one who

listens

with all my heart
and without interrupting.

(yes, really !)

What's more, I promise
I won't get carried away
with
free advice...
unless of course you
really, really want some!

In the meantime...
here's what I want you to

know,

remember,

take to heart,

memorize

and

never, ever doubt.

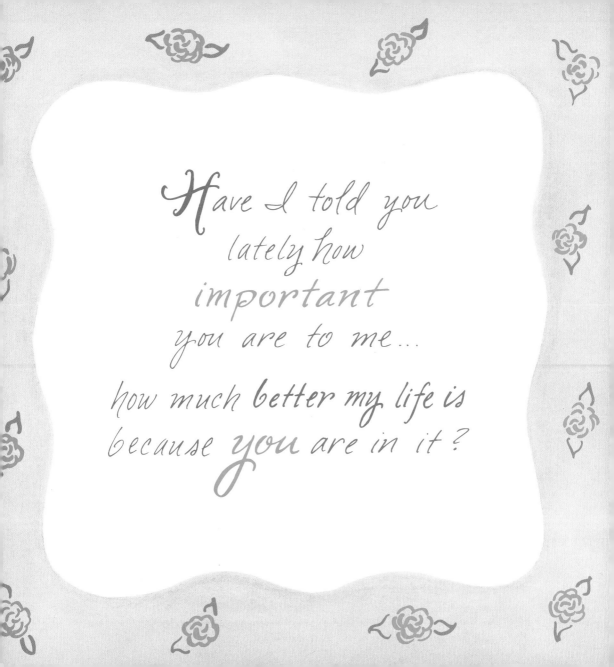

Have I told you
lately how
important
you are to me...

how much better my life is
because you are in it?

You are
kind,
compassionate,
lovely,
courageous,
intelligent,
fun,
and a
precious and spirited
friend.

I cherish you.

All the stars in the universe *danced* on the day you were born.

Imagine

There is not another you
in the whole world.
There is not another me.

We met and we became friends.

Imagine
that!

Like God's love for us,
our
friendship
is
eternal.

When I think
of you

I

smile.

Sometimes I miss
our time together,
don't you?

· creating · listening · crying · dining ·

dancing · relaxing

A TIME JUST-FOR-US

CERTIFICATE

Anytime.
Anyplace.
(your choice!)

value : priceless

talking · crafting

· gardening · laughing · walking · playing ·

One of my favorite things
about being around you is...

I get to be myself!

Wouldn't it be fun to be

Queen
for a
Day?

If you bring the tea, I'll bring the crowns!

Two
are always better than one.

Aren't we
good
together?

Don't you dare
clean
the house
before I come over!

I love you just the way you are.
Unconditionally.

I never, ever want to hurt you.

So if I ever say anything that
hurts your feelings,
please, please ask me about it because
it will make me aware
and give me the opportunity to explain.
Above all,
it will give me a chance to say
I'm sorry.

Sometimes when we're together
and it seems like we've used up
all our words,
just knowing you're near
makes me happy.

I
love how you always
seem to

understand me.

Let's plan a night in (or away!)
with our nearest and dearest friends,
a really late night (past 8:00 pm!)
with pillows and pj's (holes and all!).

We'll tell stories.
Laugh.
Celebrate friendships.
Relax, rejuvenate, and renew.

(Makes me smile just thinking about it!)

Imagine how boring
our friendship
would be if we agreed on
e v e r y t h i n g.

Instead, let's agree to
celebrate
our differences.

It's true!
One can never have enough:

___ blooming things
___ comfy shoes
___ page turners
___ yummy lingerie

Let's go shopping!

If you are ever tempted
to run away!
(and who isn't!)

think about how much
I'd miss you!

When you need to cry,
I'll be the first one
to catch your
tears.

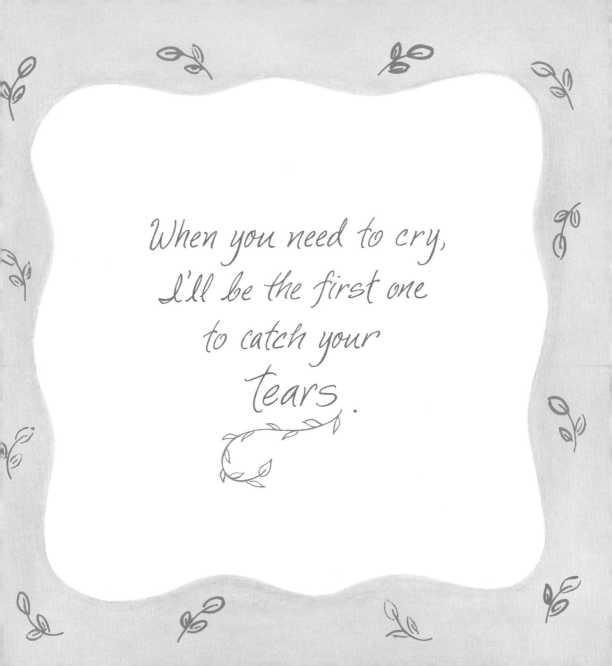

Every day
take time to
renew your spirit
with things you
love to do.

Your wholehearted joy
depends on it.

It's tough being everything to everybody.

Why not cut yourself some slack?

Let's do something just for you.

Gratitude
is a **gift** you give yourself.

So give thanks for
all the wonders that touch your days.

Fresh water.
Clean sheets.
A nap in the sun.
Spirited friends.
A bra that fits.
And what would the world
be without chocolate!

Dream. Dream. Dream.
Hold on to your dreams, dear friend.
Anything is possible.

Believe
in
yourself.

I do.

I believe
You are a very important
Somebody.

It doesn't matter if you just
won the lottery or if you have to
count every penny.

It doesn't matter if you have
it all together or if you can
never find your car keys.

It doesn't matter where you work
(or don't) or what anyone else you
know has accomplished (or not).

You are a very important
Somebody
and

I am so glad you are my friend.

Thank you for all the times you've listened without judgment...

for gently lifting my spirit with gifts of perspective...

for reminding me that things really do get better?

(But then, how could it be otherwise with you as my friend?)

Whether you are near or far,
I will always hold
our friendship
close to
my
heart.

Cherish each day.
(indulge yourself)

Play whenever you can.
(celebrate yourself)

Most of all...

take good care of yourself.

Remember to always...

eat your peas!

Why Peas?

She was a vibrant, dazzling young woman with a promising future. Yet, at sixteen, her world felt sad and hopeless.

Though I was living over 1800 miles away, I wanted to let this very special young person in my life know that I would be there for her, across the miles and through the darkness. I wanted her to know she could call me any time, at any hour, and I would be there for her. And I wanted to give her a piece of my heart that she could take with her anywhere—a reminder that she was loved.

Really loved.

Her name is Maddy, and she was the inspiration for my first book in the Eat Your Peas series, *Eat Your Peas for Young Adults.* At the very beginning of her book, I made a place to write in my phone number so she would know I was serious about being available. And right beside the phone number, I put my promise to listen—truly listen—whenever that call came.

Soon after the book was published, people began to ask me if I had the same promise and affirmation for adults. It was then that I realized it isn't just young people who need to be reminded of how truly special they are. We all do.

Today, Maddy is thriving and giving hope to others in her life. I like to think that, in some way, my book and I were part of helping her achieve that. If someone has given you this book, it means *you are a pretty amazing person to them*, and they wanted to let you know. Take it to heart.

Believe it, and remind yourself often.

Wishing you peas and plenty of joy,

Cheryl Karpen

P.S. My mama always said, "Eat your peas! They're good for you." The pages of this book are filled with nutrients for your heart. They're simply good for you too!

If this book has touched your life,
we'd love to hear your story.

Please send it to:
mystory@eatyourpeas.com
or mail it to:
Gently Spoken
PO Box 245
Anoka, MN 55303

About the author "Eat Your Peas"

A self-proclaimed dreamer, Cheryl
spends her time imagining and creating
between the historic river town of Anoka, Minnesota
and the seaside village of Islamorada, Florida.

An effervescent speaker, Cheryl brings inspiration,
insight, and humor to corporations,
professional organizations, and churches.
Learn more about her at www.cherylkarpen.com

About the illustrator

Sandy Fougner artfully weaves
a love for design, illustration and
interiors with being a wife
and mother of three sons.

With gratitude...

Every time I begin growing a new idea, I am humbled by the
knowledge that I am only one of the peas in the pod.
I only plant the seed, help nurture it and watch it grow.
Amazing people help turn my garden of dreams into a reality.

When Sandy Fougner, the illustrator of Eat Your Peas Collection,
began weaving her artistry into my gift shops and my books,
I didn't realize I would receive the greatest gift of all —
her gentle and honest friendship. Thank you, Sandy, for your passion
for Peas and for sharing your gift with girlfriends everywhere.
You are all heart and it shows.

My editor, Suzanne Foust, always makes me sound better than I really am.
You are a blessing to me, Suzanne.

A special thank you to my sister Jeanne Grams,
my dear friend Mary Lund and to all my girlfriends
who allow me to share in their lives.

~ C.K.

Other books by Cheryl Karpen

The Eat Your Peas® Collection

now available:

Eat Your Peas® for Mom
Eat Your Peas® Daughter
Eat Your Peas® New Mom
Eat Your Peas® Faithfully
Eat Your Peas® Faithfully, From Mom

To Let You Know I Care

Eat Your Peas® Girlfriend

Cover design by Koechel Peterson & Associates
Minneapolis, MN

ISBN-13: 978-1-4041-8982-9

Printed in China

11 12 13 14 15 [RRD] 5 4 3 2 1

www.thomasnelson.com